TRADING AND INVESTING SUCCESS

"The most important investment you can make is in yourself."
- Warren Buffet

TRADING: THE MINDSET TO SUCCESS

"Whatever happens, take responsibility."
- Tony Robbins

BY ELL WALKER

First Printing, 2019
ISBN: 9781097685448

To all my traders,
don't give up on your dreams.
Learn how to rest, let go and start again.
Tomorrow is a new day and
the market is still there waiting for you.

TABLE OF CONTENTS

INTRO

"Don't be afraid to give up the good to go for the great."
-John D. Rockefeller

Why you need this book......

Trading is difficult. And it's hard work, complex and risky, lonely and isolating, can create problems in marriages, destroy people's self worth and bank accounts, wipe out your retirement savings, and in extreme cases, can even drive people to suicide.

On the other side of the spectrum, it can be lifesaving, lifegiving, creating financial freedom alongside freedom from soul destroying jobs, long hours of low pay and bad conditions. It can create a different reality for yourself and for your family. It can lift someone from poverty, and it can comfort someone through retirement. But it's still difficult.

Trading is a derivative of money and it is the money that we are really in it for. Some people love the markets and naturally gravitate towards the charts, but for the most of us, we learn how to trade, how to short, put, sell and order for the reward of money. The motivation and rewards of trading will be covered later in this book, but learning how to trade is learning a skill, and no matter what any book, company, slick presenter promises you, *you will not get rich in a day* and *it is not easy*. It can be simple, but trading requires time, dedication and patience. Money doesn't grow on trees, but it can be grown.

This book is not here to teach you a strategy or help you master the QQQ, FTSE or oil. It won't tell you if fundamental or technical analysis is best and it won't tell you how to find the flips or spot a market crash; it's your job to understand the markets. Trading: the Mindset to Success was written to help you along your trading journey. From your first trade and making your $500 in profit, your thoughts, habits and mindset are crucial. If you are doubting yourself when the stakes are small, how will you ever become comfortable risking $5,000, $10,000, $50,000 on a trade? As a successful trader you will need to learn to lose money, plan across months and years and to be patient. This book will help you a plan, a goal, a strategy and a reality check, no matter where you are in your trading journey.

You need this book because without the right mindset you will never master trading.

WHO ARE YOU?

"the unexamined life is not worth living"
- Socrates

Like relationships, trading is going to show you parts of yourself you never knew about. Spending so much time with a chart and a screen can be lonely sometimes, and every trade you take will bring you a range of emotions, from excitement to despair. It's important to understand who you are and how you react to situations and integrate that into your trade plan and your personal rules. Reading the charts is only half the battle, to really become a successful trader you also need to know yourself.

YOUR PERSONALITY

Take some time to think about you as a person. Are you organised? Creative? A rule breaker and a risk taker, or do you find comfort in daily routines? Are you emotional? Do you believe your way is always correct or do you second guess everything? Are you a big picture thinker or do you dream in details? The more information you can gather on yourself the easier it will be to create routines that integrate trading into your life.

When thinking of yourself be objective and be honest. Nobody is judging your answers, and by not being truthful you are only slowing your progress down. The goal is to understand what type of trading will be best for you, and how to integrate it into your life. For example, if you are a risk taker, then you will need to integrate a risk management plan alongside clear trading rules that you stick to. When you don't stick to them, and a trade fails, then you can go back to your rules and see what went wrong. If you are risk averse, maybe you should open a demo account to practice higher levels of risk, or have a clear plan to increase exposure slowly to get comfortable with larger sum trades. If you are a little lazy, you should focus on efficiency, and if you tend to absorb as much information as possible then you should set yourself clear targets to achieve each day/week, so as not to get lost in the charts for 24 hours at a time.

If you are not sure about your personality, then these are two great tests to learn more about yourself:

http://www.personal.psu.edu/~j5j/IPIP/
https://www.16personalities.com/

There is no end of information to read and questions to ask yourself, but for the purposes of trading, the most important questions are the following:

- Are you a morning or evening person (when do you have the most energy)?
- What's your risk tolerance?
- Can I stick to a plan? Do I follow rules?
- Honestly, how much do I understand?

In the space below, try to write down an honest description of yourself.

....

....

....

....

....

....

....

....

....

....

....

WHAT'S YOUR WHY?

"He who has a why to live for can bear almost any how."
- **Viktor E. Frankl**

Another part of understanding yourself is having a clear reason to embark on a trading journey. Why do you want to trade, or why are you trading? If you want to be successful you need to understand why you are doing it in the first place, as the reason you give is going to motivate and energise you even in the toughest of times.

Money is not a strong enough why. A lot of people come to trading to get money, but it alone won't get you through the stop outs and losses. A better reason could be the things you plan on buying and why e.g. *"I want to buy my mother a house so she doesn't have to worry anymore"*, *"I want to be able to quit my job and finally feel free"*, *"I want to safeguard my family for retirement"*, or even *"I want to show the world that I made it"*. These are the why's that are going to help you persevere and ultimately succeed.

Take a moment to write out all the reasons that you are trading, and then try and find an overall why (hint, it's usually a reason that is filled with emotion).

....

....

....

....

....

....

....

....

....

....

....

....

....

....

....

What's your why? _____

Once you've found your reason to trade, write it down on your desk, frame it where you can see it daily, and calmly and patiently work toward it daily.

LIFESTYLE, JOB & FAMILY COMMITMENTS

"How you spend your days is how you spend your life"
- Annie Dillard

Part of understanding who you are is understanding your limitations. What does your every day life look like? Do you work morning shifts, on an oil rig for 5 weeks at a time? In front of a computer all day? How much spare time do you have? What family commitments do you have? How do you spend a typical week? I'm not going to ask you to track every hour of your days (although if you are interested you should read 168 Hours by Laura Vanderkam) but your trading and investing strategy should reflect your time commitments and your lifestyle.

Write down all the times in the week that you have free time:

....

....

....

....

....

....

....

....

....

....

....

From here you will be able to figure out a rough routine for trading. Don't tell yourself that you will be getting up at 5am every day to catch the market open if you are not a morning person or have to work until 11pm each night. You can only create a trading schedule from the available time you have. Again don't lie to yourself, you will only end up feeling defeated if you promise yourself time you do not have. Can you commit an hour every day - ideally at the same time of day? Or, if you hate routine, then can you commit an hour once a day? What you do in that hour will be discussed later, but the first step is to integrate trading into your life and make it your own.

Everyone's trading setup will look different depending on personality, lifestyle and why's, so it's useless to compare yourself with other people. You need to *own* your trading journey, so you need to fit it into *your* life.

WHAT YOU NEED TO SUCCEED

"There are no secrets to success. It is the result of preparation, hard work, and learning from failure."
- Colin Powell

STRATEGY

"Stop chasing the money and start chasing the passion"
- Tony Hsieh

There are thousands of different strategies on trading, each one promising something different. You can choose between technical or fundamental analysis. Should you focus on one market or trade them all? Should you safeguard, offset or hedge your bets, aim for targets or let your winners run? From scalping and day trading to building your retirement pot and credit spreads, there is too much out there to be able to do everything. Even within one market type, e.g. Foreign Exchange, there are hundreds of currency pairs, each with their own unique quirks and considerations. Without a clear strategy, beginners to trading often get lost in a whirlwind of information, jumping between assets and strategies, and are left confused and defeated. Those who jumped right in with money also end up out of pocket and feeling defeated. That's why defining your strategy from day one is essential!

The most successful trading strategy is consistency; sticking to one strategy, understanding it, then adjusting, building and developing it into your own.

There is no one magic formula, no get rich quick scheme in trading and no one is going to be able to do it all for you. Investment bankers are rich because they take a percentage of the profits, but pass all the risk onto the customers. But even they spent many years learning, listening, watching and practising their chosen strategies. They don't get to trade a million or billion dollar fund if they haven't got a proven strategy that works, and they haven't created that strategy overnight. As with everything, practice makes perfect, and it's the same with trading. Looking at the charts an hour a day and implementing your chosen strategy daily will accelerate your learning curve, build your knowledge and confidence and bring you to success much faster than dabbling in different assets, reading about different strategies and trying to copy everything out there.

It is okay to copy strategies, in fact it is a good idea to do so, but with caution. You are copying to understand, but then you need to evolve the strategy into your own. Being able to understand how a market moves, and being confident in your understanding is the key to being a good trader, and this is what sets successful traders apart. At the beginning, you will need some assistance, but over time you will need to stand alone and develop your knowledge to create your own unique strategy - this is when you will start to become successful (and probably humble).

How do you find a strategy? First, you need to know where to look. If you are a complete beginner you might need to do some reading into different assets and markets before you can start to look at strategies, but once you've chosen one, stick to it and dive into it. Take some time to answer the following questions, in order to identify an initial starting strategy.

What asset will you trade? Why?
(you may need to research time needed, time available, access, account size, mentors, information available)

....

....

....

What market will you focus on?
(max 1-2 to start, in order to fully understand seasonalities, behaviours, trends,

....

....

....

Identify 3-5 different strategies for trading that market:
(e.g. for Oil: flips, seasonal analysis, head and shoulders formations, world news)

....

....

....

Potential mentors to help:
(this could be a friend, an author of a book, instructor of a course, or even a youtube blogger. The key to finding a mentor is finding someone who is an advanced trader and who resonates with you, helping to make their strategy understandable. When you find a mentor, read/watch/listen to everything they say)

....

....

....

Based on the answers to the above sections, what is your trading strategy?
(e.g. I will look for seasonal moves on oil and coffee futures, I will follow moves of 50 pips or more on 3 different dollar pairs in forex.)

....

....

....

Now that you have a starting point, you can start to build a plan.

PLAN

*"I find that the harder I work,
the more luck I seem to have."*
- **Thomas Jefferson**

After you identify the strategy you will take, the next step is to make a plan. Because you have now chosen something to follow and adapt, you can now plan it into your life and plan for success. Your plan should reflect the asset(s) you are trading, your lifestyle, time availability, and personality type. It should also cover your trading journey in detail, from how long you will study, how long you use a demo account before you go live, when will you look for potential trades, how much you will risk per trade, number of open and pending trades you will take and for how long you will keep them open. The more detail you add to your plan the easier your trading journey will become, and more confident you will become. This is because you are taking away all uncertainty and emotions from trading, and reducing trades down to a simple equation; does this trade meet or break my rules?

Having a plan and being able to stick to it is incredibly important for every achievement in life. Abraham Lincoln once said, "give me six hours to chop down a tree and I will spend the first four sharpening the axe." It is the same for trading, it's better to prepare before doing in order to conserve energy. If you end up jumping straight into trades, you won't understand what's happening, or where you are going wrong. But if you were able to say, 'I took X trades looking for Y pattern, and it seems they all stopped up because of Z', now you are able to refine and adjust your strategy!

Good plans are well thought out and can be upwards of 10 pages of rules. Following and including all aspects of this book should help you create a good basic plan that you can adapt as necessary. This chapter, *what you need to succeed*, includes everything you need to prepare to embark on a successful journey, and each heading offers an aspect to consider. What you need to figure out is your individual circumstances and how *your* strategy and *your* plan look. You may wonder why the emphasis is on *you*, but it is because you have to go through the steps to develop the mindset and skills needed. Just like a language, no one can do it for you, to be able to understand and speak, you will need to put in the hours and effort to learn, but in time you will be rewarded with the ability to communicate in that language (or reap the rewards of trading).

A trade plan is best written from scratch, so no space is included here. Once you have finished reading through this book, use the contents page as a guideline for different headings, and take your time to write your answers down and create your trading plan.

GOAL

"Without a goal, you can't score"
- **Casey Neistat**

Do you want to get rich trading? How rich? Do you want to improve the quality of life - how so? Want to quit your job? Well, how much money do you need to make monthly to support your outgoings? These are all things to consider and relate closely to your why discussed in the previous section. Goals can be incredibly motivating and act as a compass guiding you to where you want to go. They also act as stepping stones to help you succeed faster.

Goals can be large or small, daily, weekly, yearly or even the near impossible. For example, Jane wants to run a marathon in 5 hours. She can break her goal down into smaller, more manageable goals, that will help her eventually run the marathon. Once a month she could run a half marathon in under 2.5 hours, and weekly, she needs to run at least 30 km (so 3 days a week she should run 10km). Breaking down the marathon goal into smaller, realistic chunks will help Jane get there. A good way to create goals is with the SMART method:

S - specific (run a marathon in 5 hours, grow my account to $20,000)
M - measurable (average speed, number of runs per week, $5,000 account into $20,000)
A - achievable (Jane could do this in 6-9 months, Joe has 10 hours a week dedicated to trading and has a strategy and a plan)
R - realistic (Jane loves running and is semi-fit, trading contributes to my overall life plan)
T - timebound (Paris marathon on Saturday 3rd November, account doubled in 12 months)

Be realistic with where you are at in your trading journey, and how you will get there. Make sure your goals contribute to your overall reason why, and also match your personality (e.g. running every morning at 6am won't work if you aren't a morning person, trading the market open won't work if you have to be at work during that time).

Now try writing your goals down:

• In one years time……..

....

....

....

....

- To reach this goal, every month I will……

....

....

....

....

- Every week I will……

....

....

....

....

- Every day I will…….

....

....

....

....

How is my goal:

Specific:

....

....

Measurable:

....

....

Achievable:

....

....

Realistic:

....

....

Timebound:

....

....

Once you are confident with your goal, write it on a post-it and stick it above your computer screen, frame it or add it to your phone's home screen picture. Seeing it every day and working towards it daily will help you get closer to it. It's even worth keeping a notebook and daily reflecting on what you did to get towards your goal, or if you didn't, what stopped you. Once you have defined a goal it will be a lot easier to achieve it because you can aim at it and move towards it every day.

TIME AND DEDICATION

It might seem easy in theory to set aside an hour a day to look at a chart and place a trade, but in practice, it's harder than it seems. Ask anyone who tried to start a gym routine, learn a new language or learn anything. Thinking about doing something, and actually doing something are two different things.

Committing to trading daily is akin to building a muscle, you need to learn how to build a habit, and in order to do that you need to do something consistently and with a goal and a plan. How many hours can you commit per week to trading? Find a way to build it into your routine, and try to do it the same time every day. For example, if you take public transport to work, are you able to analyse a chart on your way to work? Could you look at a market open over coffee? Or spend 20 minutes after you put the kids to bed at night? There is always some time available, even if you are trading to free up more time, drop the things that aren't important (like scrolling on Facebook or watching Netflix).

For those stretched for time, the hardest thing about trading is being able to sit down at the computer and start. If you block time out and put it into your daily schedule, then it forces you to be accountable and show up. 20 minutes a day might not sound a lot, but over time it adds up. And once you sit down and start analysing charts, suddenly you will find more time, as momentum and motivation will build up.

So when will you trade? How many days a week? How long for?

....

....

....

....

....

....

After clearing time for trading, you need to be very clear with what you will do during it. Trading is excellent for wasting time, staring at charts and reading around all the different strategies and voices of the internet. If you are dedicating 20 minutes a day, maybe you can go through the motions and place a trade on the oil market in 20 minutes. Or maybe you can analyse the trends of 3 forex pairs. Maybe in 30 minutes you could do both. Whatever you decide to do, it must contribute towards your smaller and larger goals (as outlined earlier) and fit into your plan. It's important to think of efficiency when it comes to trading as there is so much information out there, you can easily fall down the rabbit hole and waste precious trading time. Set clear goals for each chunk of time you've blacked out and hopefully you'll be able to make large steps towards your trading goals. Start by figuring out what you 'need to know'. This will help you streamline your thoughts and use your time efficiently, as you will have a list of things to learn. Work out how long things will take, and if they take longer, then plan a little extra time the following week to get there. Don't forget to have patience with yourself. Learning a language comes in stages, from finally understanding words, to broken conversations, new vocabulary and finally mastery. Trading is the same. There are lots of different fragments to discover, and some of them you might not even realise you are missing until you find them. It's all the road to trading mastery.

During the time you've set aside, what will you do?

....

....

....

....

....

....

PRACTICE

Practice makes perfect
- anonymous

In his book Outliers, author Malcolm Gladwell explains the 10,000 hour rule, whereby practising something for enough hours makes you a success in any field. If you break the number down, it equates to 20 hours a week for 10 years or an average decade of a career. This idea has been challenged by many others, citing that it isn't only the time that counts, but also the quality of the practice that matters.

Regardless of how many exact hours make you an expert at something, the more time you spend on it, the better you will get at it. Trading is no different; if you put the hours in, and spend the time needed to analyse, adapt and evolve your strategy, then there is no doubt you will improve. Don't expect to become a profitable trader overnight, but you will be a good trader after a year of effort, and a profitable one if you can add the quality element to your trading. How do you do that? By taking ownership of your trading journey, tracking and regularly analysing trades and markets for patterns, and by taking a step back sometimes to see the bigger picture.

It's wise to find an accountability partner, a mentor or even a coach once you start to get into the swing of trading, as it can help take you to the next level. Tony Robbins is a coach that works with some of the most successful people in the world, as even they have elements they can improve on, and trading is no different. At the start of the journey, you will often need to put the hours in, but as you become more confident and comfortable with the markets, you can get help with the quality of your work through a trading group or a coach. Investment bankers have coaches, mentors, colleagues and a boss to help them. Visit www.trading-mindset-success.com if you are interested in finding out more.

As well as practice, you should think about perseverance. It's not easy to turn up in front of the charts every day, trade and learn. Every day - that's a lot of stamina. It's natural to sometimes take a break or skip a day, as long as you keep your *why* and *goals* in mind. It's not easy to turn up in front of the computer every day, especially if you are experiencing some losing trades, and some people quit during the hard times. However, it is natural to take losses in trading, just make sure that you have included risk management in your plan.

When breaking your goals into smaller chunks, don't forget to also include rewards when you achieve them. As a beginner, if you manage to take a trade a day for 5 days in a row, reward yourself with something nice, regardless of if the trades were successful or not - you are still building the habit and creating a positive association towards trading. As you achieve more goals, make your rewards bigger (but not at the expense of your account size). You deserve rewards for your work, and the money will come after the time and perseverance you've initially put into your trading.

PAPER TRAIL

"Many of life's failures are people who did not realize how close they were to success when they gave up."
-Thomas Edison

No matter how you record your trades, it's essential to have a 'paper' trail of what you've been doing. All trading platforms will be able to give you a list of trades taken, and the results of those trades, but don't rely on this, it's not enough. What you need are records, photos, screenshots, lists, excel sheets, anything that you are later able to look back upon as a history of what you've done. The easiest way to start is to create an excel sheet with the following: market, entry, target, stop, information on how it met your strategy/rules, result (profitable or not), and an accompanying picture for later analysis. After a month, sometimes even a day of trading, you will not remember what trades you took or the reasons why. Hopefully, you will have had a profitable trade, but regardless, you can analyse the trade and learn from it. Eventually, you will see patterns in profitable trades, or in the losses, and then can adjust your strategy based on the information you recorded.

At first logging all your trades might feel difficult, but to get to the end of a month with nothing but a loss is much more frustrating. The more information you have collected the faster you will become a stronger trader as you can look objectively at what you have been doing.

Another great paper trail is a handwritten journal. Plan your days in it, log your screen time, trades and emotions in it and watch your trading journey fill the pages. Trading can bring up a whole range of emotions and so it's good to have an outlet to write away your frustrations. A trading journal is another great way to gather information, accelerate your learning and track your trading. It's also helpful when you are looking for advice on how to make your trading stronger, as no one can help you unless they can see where you are going wrong. A journal might highlight small mistakes you are making, common thought patterns and negative self-talk that might be holding you back. It might take time to become aware of negative thoughts or patterns, but once you do your trading (and your outlook on life) will elevate to a higher level.

Questions to answer in your journal include:
-   What happened in this trade to make a profitable/losing trade?
-   What did I see that made me want to take this trade?
-   How was I feeling at the time? Did I follow my rules?
-   Do I trust my initial analysis now that I've looked at it again?
-   How do I feel about the day?

REALITY CHECK

---

*"Lying to ourselves is more deeply ingrained
than lying to others."*
- Fyodor Dostoevsky

Before we go any further, it is worth taking a break and going back to reread the notes you have taken. Is it all realistic? Are you really going to put in 30 hours of trading a week (just to get to Malcolm Gladwell's definition of success faster)? Is your first goal a little too audacious? Is your plan a little weak, the time you blocked out structured enough, your husband or wife interested in being your accountability partner? We all want to become professional, successful and profitable traders, but don't forget that every trader once started from scratch (just like you). Your plan needs to be long term and your goals SMART. Your strategy will inevitably evolve, but your reason why should be present every day you sit down and trade. Don't over promise things to yourself or others, but make sure everything is achievable and realistic - this will put you in line for the long term and overall more profitable.

When you think of yourself on your trading journey, make note of the story you tell yourself. Are you exhausted just thinking about it, scared you won't get it because you are not a numbers person, or lost money through trades in the past? Some of us carry negative internal feedback stories, that can cause negative feedback loops. These tend to be larger than just one failed trade. How you do see yourself? As a winner or a loser? This stems all the way back to childhood, school and parents. Taking small steps, and celebrating small wins, along with positive internal feedback is key to you persevering. If possible, catch the phrases that cause a poor self-image, and try to replace them with positive statements instead. Don't say, "I can't do this, it's too hard", swap it with, "I'm learning so much every day, showing up and working towards my dreams. I am will get there when I am ready, but I will get there".

BEGINNER PROBLEMS

"The best time to plant a tree was twenty years ago. The second best time is today"
- Chinese proverb

Congratulations on making the first steps on your trading journey. The learning curve may be steep, the emotional one even steeper, but you are actively taking steps towards your goals and your ultimate reason for learning to trade - this alone should make you feel really proud! You are following your dreams, and there is never a better time to start than today, but your dreams are also hard work and it takes time to achieve them, so don't give up if you have a couple of stop outs, focus on how happy you will be in 5 years time being consistently profitable.

Below are the seven issues beginners need to accept, address and overcome to become profitable and successful traders.

UNDERSTANDING

At the very basic level of trading, you need to understand yourself and your strategy. You don't necessarily need to understand the markets or even why they are moving, you just need to know that your strategy works. To do this you need to believe, but in order for you to believe you must first find data from the charts to verify your strategy works. Test the history of the charts, demo trade your strategy, live trade smaller amounts to start (always use a stop), and get used to the feeling that comes with trading.

When you are a new trader you have to deal with a lot of feelings, so it's wise to take each step slowly and calmly. Don't think about missed profit, focus on the process. Missed profits can make us go crazy, make rash moves and silly mistakes, so tell yourself they weren't yours to have; you don't deserve them yet but you will get to a level when you will catch them all.

As well as believing in your strategy, you need to learn who to trust. Banks, newspapers, financial advisors, even friends all have their own way of seeing things, and so you can't trust them. It might take time not to panic when the news is screaming about the S&P going down, but watch the aftermath, where it dips and ends up going higher than before. If a trade doesn't fit your strategy or your plan, then don't take it, especially when you are influenced by outside voices. Don't be the novice asking for 'tips' or 'what market to choose', they don't win in the short or long run. Be the trader who tests, analyses, adjusts and tests their strategies. The trader who is confident and self-assured in their plan, strategy, goal and actions. This is how you become successful.

MISTAKES

"Would you like me to give you a formula for success? It's quite simple, really: Double your rate of failure. You are thinking of failure as the enemy of success. But it isn't at all. You can be discouraged by failure or you can learn from it, so go ahead and make mistakes. Make all you can. Because remember that's where you will find success."
- Thomas J. Watson

Mistakes happen and are all part of a learning curve, so instead of beating yourself up when you make them, learn from them and integrate them into your strategy so you don't make them again. When you make a mistake, include it in your journal, with information on what you saw, what you were thinking and what actually happened. Look at the chart pattern again to break down what you saw and what you missed. No one likes to make mistakes, but think of them as stepping stones on your journey; if you look at them, they will help you get to your goal faster.

Another problem are profitable trades that didn't follow your rules. Trades taken with random levels and no plan are not going to make you a successful trader. You might have made some profit from them, but this is money make by mistake and should be classed as gambling, not trading. Money made by mistake is like taking a loss - you didn't learn and can't replicate it so will end up giving that money back to the markets at a later date. Any professional trader will tell you that as a beginner, if your first few trades are successful you will end up losing a lot more in the markets because of false self-confidence.

SELF-SABOTAGE

Self-sabotage appears differently in everyone. Some people are fearful and so lose trades from self-doubt, others will over risk and take rash decisions as they like to 'live on the edge', or 'take advantage of every opportunity in life'. These ideas are embedded into each of us and link closely to the first section of this book - Who are you? You need to be particularly watchful of your own behaviour in the first few months of trading to see what self-sabotaging ideas come up. Each are unique and sometimes hard to spot, which is why keeping a journal and writing down your emotional state at the time is incredibly helpful. Following your strategy and rules exactly is the best way to minimise risk and self-sabotage, as it takes a certain level of subjectiveness out of the equation.

Other self-sabotaging ideas that may come up include; *I have to make money today, big position sizes mean big money, the more I trade the more opportunities I have, stops are not needed because I am right, I will place one more trade to make up for the previous loss.* These are all incredibly common thoughts and need to be addressed as soon as they are thought, otherwise they will end up losing you money. Markets and data are objective facts, but it is us that brings the human emotional element into trading. A trade either worked or it didn't, and it is your strategy that needs to be adjusted in order to fit the market.

PATIENCE

"A man who masters patience masters everything"
- anonymous

Of all the things to cultivate in trading, the most important one is patience. Patience will overcome all the other emotions, especially fear, excitement, elation, greed, self-doubt and apathy. Patience will help you though when you are thinking of giving up, or when you can't find a trade that meets your rules, when you are watching your account balance increase slower than expected, or when we want to impulse trade. It's the breathe in, breathe out habit that can help reign in all our emotions, and it's one of the best tools we have as a beginner trader.

Hopefully, by spending some time at the start of this book self-reflecting on your personality and who you are, you will have realised how patient you are. Another aspect to consider is how you are good at following rules, as the rules you have added to your plan are the framework that will help you become a successful trader. If you are naturally a rule breaker, then this should be high on your priorities to avoid, or at least track, in order to avoid breaking your plan. You can't break the rules until you know how they work, so you need to be patient and reign in your bad habits. Take some time to write in your journal why you feel the need to break rules - perhaps it stems from a disregard for authority in your childhood, or maybe you think some rules are stupid. Whatever it is, it is only going to hurt you and your account in the long run so you need to be more patient with yourself. One way of avoiding breaking your rules is to pay more attention to the initial process of setting trades, and then walking away and doing something else. If you aren't able to access your trade, then you can't adjust anything and so you let it run naturally. Whatever your bad habits are, you need the patience to get over them and become a successful trader. And whoever said traders weren't emotional?

RESULTS

After a whole book of things to consider we can finally start talking about the things that matter - results. We all want profitable results, but when it comes to trading profitable trades come hand in hand with failed trades. The trick to looking at results is across a larger time frame, months or years, not daily or weekly. Yes maybe you had a week of trades that went the wrong way to what you thought, but as long as your month has been positive then those days are all part of the larger picture. Some people experience many stop outs before they hit a string of successes, and so patience, belief in the strategy and tracking all trades taken are important to show you the overall results.

As mentioned before, it's essential to track your results as this will help to show you what you have done, where you need to adjust or change a strategy, what is working and what isn't. Some people like to write their trades down on paper, others in excel, many like to screenshot trade order windows, or the chart itself. Anything works, just make sure you have that paper trail to show you what you've been doing so that you can go back and review. Your results will be the thing that grows your account over time.

Another reason to track your results is to see if losing trades are hurting your account. You will take losing trades, this is inevitable, and it's normal. Depending on your risk to reward, you can afford to take lots of losing trades as long as you are taking a few winning ones. For example, if your risk to reward is 4:1 then you can afford to take 4 losing trades for every winning trade, and so only need to be right 1/5 of the time, or just over 20%. If you find you are averaging more losses to wins, then you can adjust your risk to reward ratio. If most of your trades are profitable then your account size will be growing quite fast. You just need to be comfortable will losing trades, as it's all part of the process.

MONEY

"Too many people spend money they earned..to buy things they don't want..to impress people that they don't like"
-Will Rogers

As your account starts to grow don't immediately start spending. Focus back on your goals and your why. Write down some numbers and track the percentage growth you are making month by month. These days banks offer savers between 0.1% and 2% interest. Rental property averages a return of around 5-7% per year, as do hedge funds and indexes. Stocks can increase in value, but their yearly dividends are miniscule unless you have thousands of shares.

Trading however, can bring you returns of 50%, 100%, 1000% returns within a year (and that's with a fair amount of failed trades). 100% return on $5,000 is $5,000. At the end of year one you have $10,000, then if you take out $5,000 the following year your 100% return brings you back to the same figure. If you don't touch your account, and let it compound, then after year two your account will be $20,000 ($10,000 after year 1 x 100%). After a few years, not only will your account have grown substantially, but you will also have improved as a trader and so are making more successful trades. There will be a time to spend all your profits, but for now focus on your goals and on your trades.

THE FUTURE

"Happiness is not in the mere possession of money; it lies in the joy of achievement, in the thrill of creative effort"
-Franklin D. Roosevelt

Trading is something that follows you throughout your life. It isn't something you use for a day or two, or learn in a few weeks, rather it is a skill that gets honed and sharpened over time. Many novice traders forget that, and when the going gets tough, they give up. It's important to understand that the first year of trading will be the hardest time you will have with the markets - there is so much to learn, so many mistakes to make, so many things to understand, try and master. In your second year you will become more consistent and start to make progress, and from year 3 onwards you should hopefully be flying to the moon. There will be more issues to face as you become more profitable, but they will rear their heads when you get there, but for now the focus for beginners needs to be adopting trading into your life and making room for it. It isn't easy, and it definitely isn't a get rich quick scheme, but over time trading becomes simple and enjoyable, and that's where the real profits live. When you dream of your future be sure to include trading in it, as this will allow you to be truly successful throughout your life.

CONCLUSION

"Wealth is the ability to fully experience life"
-Henry David Thoreau

Well done on taking the first steps on your trading journey, and thanks for allowing me to be part of your journey. Many of us come to trading because we want more from life. It isn't just about the money, it's about the things we can do with money. Improve the quality of life for ourselves and others, find more time, and become able to fully experience life. Money is only a means to an end, and the true test is what we do with it. Your goals and your reason why will help you more than anything else in this journey, as these will be your energy, your motivation and your willpower to keep going.

If you found this book useful, please take the time to leave me a review and five stars on amazon. Also gift this book to anyone who might need a little extra help with their trading - good karma brings peace and success in all areas of your life.

If you have further questions, please don't hesitate to send a message or ask for help via https://www.trading-mindset-success.com/.

I wish you every success on your trading journey. Now go write that trading plan!

- Ell W.